I Too Once Thought . . .

I Too Once Thought . . .

Problematizing Identity and Ordering the So-Called Chaos in Alanis Morissette's *Supposed Former Infatuation Junkie*

BRETT ALAN DEWING

RESOURCE *Publications* • Eugene, Oregon

I TOO ONCE THOUGHT...
Problematizing Identity and Ordering the So-Called Chaos in Alanis Morissette's *Supposed Former Infatuation Junkie*

Copyright © 2026 Brett Alan Dewing. All rights reserved. Except for brief quotations in critical publications or reviews, no part of this book may be reproduced in any manner without prior written permission from the publisher. Write: Permissions, Wipf and Stock Publishers, 199 W. 8th Ave., Suite 3, Eugene, OR 97401.

Resource Publications
An Imprint of Wipf and Stock Publishers
199 W. 8th Ave., Suite 3
Eugene, OR 97401

www.wipfandstock.com

PAPERBACK ISBN: 979-8-3852-5400-2
HARDCOVER ISBN: 979-8-3852-5401-9
EBOOK ISBN: 979-8-3852-5402-6

01/23/26

Scripture quotations taken from The Holy Bible, New International Version®, NIV®. Copyright © 1973, 1978, 1984, 2011 by Biblica, Inc. Used with permission of Zondervan. All rights reserved worldwide. www.zondervan.com

The author would like to thank India, terror, disillusionment, frailty, consequence, silence, providence, nothingness, and clarity.

Contents

These R My Thoughts | 1
Title & Cover Art | 4
"Front Row" | 8
"Baba" | 12
"Thank U" | 15
"Are You Still Mad" | 18
"Sympathetic Character" | 21
"That I Would Be Good" | 24
"The Couch" | 27
"Can't Not" | 31
"UR" | 34
"I Was Hoping" | 36
"One" | 40
"Would Not Come" | 43
"Unsent" | 46
"So Pure" | 48
"Joining You" | 50
"Heart of the House" | 53
"Your Congratulations" | 55
Conclusion | 58
Bibliography | 61

These R My Thoughts

EVEN AN INITIAL LISTEN through Alanis Morissette's seventeen-track sophomore American album, *Supposed Former Infatuation Junkie*, will bring three formal techniques to the foreground. In a bold evolution of the singer/songwriter's style and a significant departure from the radio hits of the era, Morissette's 1998 album almost obsessively doubles down on elements already obvious on her breakthrough collection, *Jagged Little Pill*: stacking, repetition, and listing. Considering the album's spiritual concerns and almost ritualistic structure, I feel justified in suggesting we think about these binding principles as The Three Ls: layering, liturgy, and litany.

From the very beginning, the musical layering of *SFIJ* is clear. The aural signature of the work is built with sounds and instruments from a wide variety of traditions and cultures. The album not only layers sounds into thick soundscapes; it also layers thoughts. In many of the litany songs, the parallel structure of the introductory phrases ("How about . . . ," "That I would be . . . ," "I was afraid of . . . ") create a canvas onto which the completing phrases stack up, creating a thematic palimpsest as well as a sonic one. We will also see how Alanis explores her own multiplicity through layers of her own voice singing different parts. This creates a chorus of Alanises (Alanii? Alanes?) representing different personas/iterations/parts of the woman at the album's complicated core. This should immediately remind any fan of the music video for "Ironic" (from *Jagged Little Pill*), in which four versions of

I Too Once Thought . . .

the singer are joyriding in a car, or the video for "Reasons Why I Drink" (from *Such Pretty Forks in the Road*), which features a support group of different Alanises.

The liturgy of the album is embodied through repetition that can be musical or lyrical or both. This is done by taking a short phrase—be it a musical or grammatical one—and building the song through its repetition. Some songs, such as "Unsent," approach this concept by the looping of a musical phrase that Alanis fills with cornucopias of words. The very fecundity of the lyrics on the album, and the ways in which they are manipulated in strange ways to fit into the melodies, create the brimming-over effect which suffuses the album and speaks to its theme of complication and complexity—of myriad ideas filling the same spaces. Other songs, such as "That I Would Be Good," work around an introductory linguistic phrase that is paired with a series of completing phrases. Both tactics are often in play at the same time, however, with tracks like "I Was Hoping" using musical liturgy in the verses and textual liturgy in the chorus.

Our third L—litany—arises as a consequence of the other two. Almost every song uses a listing technique, whether it be a list of revelatory observations about would-be Buddhists ("Baba") or a list of different reactions to the process of talk therapy ("The Couch"). Litany is always at the core of Morissette's songwriting, no matter the album. She is less often interested in delivering a narrative through her lyrics than she is of, shall we say, keeping the books (the very books referred to at the start of "UR"): she gathers evidence without overtly interpreting it for us.

All three of these techniques are used in the service of problematizing our concept of single and monolithic identity and the attempt to overlay chaos with some kind of order. Here, it can be helpful to cite two phrases Morissette has used in talking about her music and personal journey: "bothness" and "All Parts." "Bothness" means the fight to be seen as a realistically complex human who is both strong and weak, kind and cruel. This goes against our cultural grain, as we are quick to label people and slot them away in their cubbyholes. There is great power and freedom in acknowledging our sometimes-contradictory natures—especially as fallen beings made in God's image. "All Parts" is a refrain Alanis often uses in her personal diaries. A similar idea to "bothness," this philosophy intersects with the branch of psychology called Internal Family Systems. Inside of us, it says, there is a family. (Inside our car, there are four Alanises.) These different aspects of oneself relate to each other in many complex ways. A common struggle, for example, is between one's protective parts and one's wounded parts. IFS celebrates the multiplicity of identity, empowering a central Self figure who is in interaction with their parts, which have often (as in a family) been forced into extreme or reactionary stances by the circumstances of life.

Supposed Former Infatuation Junkie is Alanis's "Song of Myselves," her wild yawp, her portrait of the artist as a multitude. As we make a close reading of each song on the album (as well as the title and cover image), we will constantly be coming back to the Three Ls, "bothness," and "All Parts" as well a growing focus on spirituality and the tenants of Internal Family Systems.

Title & Cover Art

THE MOST IMPORTANT ELEMENTS of a linguistic art piece (a novel, play, story, anthology, etc.) are its title and its first and last lines. In a fictional piece, names are also of priority importance. With a musical album, we may add the art that has been chosen for the cover, as this should work as a sort of visual title, cohering with all elements while putting some of the album's central themes or moods into conversation. (And, unlike the proverbial book, this cover does not change over time or distance, making it a more reliable way to judge what is within.)

Therefore, we can point to the following as the parts of a pop album we should discuss first:

- Title
- First song
- First lyric
- Last song
- Last lyric
- Song titles
- Cover art

Let me start with the title and cover art.

The phrase *"Supposed Former Infatuation Junkie"* has one immediate effect: it is an unusually long album title (this side of Fiona

Title & Cover Art

Apple). Already, we are submerged in the dominant tone and form of the album. These songs are overflowing with lyrics, just as their orchestrations give a similar effect through extensive layering. Looking at the album as a self-portrait, the message we might infer from this technique is that "I am legion"—or, less demonically, "I contain multitudes."

Through the abundance of words (almost five thousand across seventeen songs), Alanis is saying something like, "If all the things that I could call myself were listed here, no book would be able to hold them. The more I try to describe what I see in the mind's mirror, the more I notice smaller brushstrokes, wayward spots of color, inverse shapes, and ever more complex patterns."

A second thing to note about the title is that it is an identity statement, a self-naming. What will we find in this collection? A supposed former infatuation junkie—not just the thoughts of one. Grammatically dissecting the phrase, we find that identity further complicated. She is a "junkie": perhaps we should not be surprised by the manic chain of words. Her drug is "infatuation": this is by nature a passing state, unlike (for example) love. But wait—that label is modified twice more, acknowledging that this self-label is already "former" (her addiction to the temporary rush of infatuation has proved itself temporary) and "supposed" (this description was placed upon her by another, and its veracity is still up in the air). In trying to name herself, she must resort to the perceptions of others, unverified information, and the fact that by the time the label is given, it no longer applies.

This is already a dizzying complication of identity created by a litany of clarifying adjectives (that might not really be clarifying much of anything)!

The second theme this book discusses in the album—ordering the world's/self's chaos—is illustrated by the photo on the album's cover. We see two superimposed images: an extreme closeup of the singer's mouth laughing and a list of rules which includes the injunction "please refrain from. . .playing music, singing. . .." (Notice the bothness of this dual image.)

I Too Once Thought . . .

The first image is important not just because it is a literal portrait of Alanis but because it is her mouth, out of which all these words have come . . . and perhaps continue to come. After all, couldn't that laughing mouth be instead singing? Either way, it is wide open, in the act of creating some sound. We must also pay attention to the fact that this closeup of the mouth is very obviously only a part of a face/human/identity, being examined very closely. The same technique will show up in the lyrics.

The cover's other image—the litany of rules—holds an equal opacity with that of the mouth. While the viewer's first thought may likely be that the singer is laughing at the restrictions on the sign, I ask you to also consider it in reverse: the chaos of uncontrolled laughter is overlaid with an ordered list of words which form a social code. Could it be that the rules are in fact imposed over the mouth in an attempt to provide structure and order? (And what does it suggest that the text of the sign contains spelling errors?)

As it turns out, these are not just random rules. They are in the style of (and sometimes quote) Buddhism's five precepts. With this in mind, it is even more compelling to believe that the words are taming the chaos of the chaotic human, and not the mouth laughing at the words. (Or perhaps the song "Baba" might suggest that it is a little of both?)

We will look at each song's title in its corresponding chapter, but it is worth setting down the first and last titles/lines. The album opens with "Front Row" and closes with "Your Congratulations." Both of these phrases conjure images of performance and interaction. They carry an aura of theatricality and may be related to the audience in the front row congratulating the person onstage for the performance of their character/identity.

The first and last lines of the album are equally compelling when set side by side. The first words we hear state, "I know he's blood, but you can still turn him away; you don't owe him anything." The last are "It was your approval I wanted, your congratulations." Both lyrics deal with interpersonal relationships. We will see that "Your Congratulations" is almost certainly about Alanis's father. This adds to the effect by identifying each line with blood

Title & Cover Art

relatives. In the opening line, someone (perhaps the singer) is contemplating turning a relative away. In the last, it appears that a close relative (her father) has turned away from her. This is similar to the ways in which Internal Family Systems talks about rifts in our inner families. And yet, we are given access to both viewpoints: All Parts.

"Front Row"

ALANIS WASTES NO TIME in plunging us beneath the waters of her album. "Front Row" immediately drowns the listener in dense sonic layering and a forest of lyrics. (Unfortunately, in order to protect Morissette's copyright, I cannot print the full lyrics here in all their glory. I strongly suggest finding an online source for each song's lyrics before reading the corresponding chapter. Even if you stream the songs, you may have trouble taking in the avalanche of lyrics.) Words are even layered on top of words. For example, the last three lines of the fourth verse all overlap parts of each other, making it hard to put the thoughts in sequence. Even more disorienting is the way each chorus covers over a half dozen lines, which are functionally impossible to discern without a sheet of lyrics before you. (Even then, I can only hear a scattering of the words.)

This is not a wall of sound but more like a biosphere of sound, as the multiplicity of the music and lyrics are always somehow working together to tell a complex story, one that unfolds in the tree canopy as much as on the forest floor and all the spaces in between. Truly, the singer has put you in the front row of her new sound with no warning. After decades of listening, I still can't catch all of the uppermost lyrics, let alone those buried beneath the chorus. (The song stops short of creating a litany, but it does talk about the singer and her subject making a list of "thirty good reasons we shouldn't be together.")

This opening salvo of a long, truly unique album works well for our purposes, too. It is a clear and widespread example of All Parts. We see bothness represented in her subject's contradictory impressions, which she even labels "Jekyll and Hydeness." Morissette does not feel any simple admiration for her subject. She swings from resentment to desire to empathy to anger.... Truly, what she loves about this man is everything—All Parts—and she experiences this love through All Parts of herself.

This is not only a refreshingly realistic display of the complexity of identity but also of the multivalent nature of true relationship. It is often a stumbling block for fallen humans to believe that God loves their every part. How can he even pull that off? Here, Alanis shows us how close we come in even our human relationships. How much more can we rest in the fact that God can love our "unlovable" parts?

Biographically, we know that this song comes from multiple conversations Morissette had with filmmaker Kevin Smith while appearing his 1999 film, *Dogma*. It is a film that, to me, always comes off as trying very hard to scandalize the Roman Catholic Church but never actually succeeding. In fact, the film has things to teach American Christians, especially regarding representations of God.

Morissette herself plays God in the film. (Notice the double meaning at the end of the first verse, when she wants the man to be "kissed by God.") At that time, in the full bloom of her reputation as "that angry singer who uses the f-word," this was clearly a controversial casting choice. Her womanhood alone is too much for many Christians, and I would agree if she were portraying Christ specifically. However, she is representing the entire Godhead, which has qualities that humans would call masculine and feminine. And while I hope that we can all agree that anger is not a trait foreign to the Father, Morissette's performance is one of absolute wordless joy in all of Creation. When I need to be reminded of God's playfulness, I often remember Alanis doing cartwheels among the wildflowers.

It is vital, however, to take this version of the character "God" along with the movie's most enduring and insightful creation:

I Too Once Thought . . .

Buddy Christ. Buddy Christ is a statue or image of a conventionally portrayed Jesus who is simultaneously giving the thumbs up, winking, and jovially pointing with a "there he is!" smile. Here, Smith has hit the nail directly on the head. This version of Jesus is still propagated by the American church. He is constantly encouraging, never really serious, and always pointing at you, not himself. Calvary is unimaginable in the culture of Buddy Christ, thereby taking the very core of our faith and divesting him of his reason for being. While I never liked *Dogma*, I am thankful to Kevin Smith for his takedown of Buddy Christ. (If only more Christians could get past a female God long enough to notice the dire implications of a Buddy Jesus.)

All of that background is in some ways outside of the song "Front Row," but as the album and film came out within months of each other, I think the connections were meant to be one more layer of covered-up dialogue.

Returning to the lyrics, I would like to point out a few things before we move on to the next song. Remember my description of the photograph of Morissette's mouth on the cover while you glance over the words of the chorus. Remember the self-labelling title of the album. *Supposed Former Infatuation Junkie* is our chance to see Alanis "close up." Next, take note of the bothness of Morissette's lyrics: in a conversational voice, they run through Shakespeare allusions and *mea culpas* amid their stream-of-consciousness wanderings. She is a songwriter who can put forth the seemingly unordered at the same time as the tightly formatted along with objective and subjective points of view that belie the high art/low art dichotomy.

While "Front Row" gives us a wealth of lyrical content to consider, I am exploring the way in which it works as a perfect opening track, giving us an idea of the album's medium and message. I will, then, only draw acute attention to the beginning of the first verse.

> Do you go to the dungeon
> To find out how to make peace
> With your days in the dungeon?

"Front Row"

This is another great introductory sentence. Is the only way to heal the trauma of our pasts to go through it again? Fittingly, this healing and revisiting are major concerns of the album. And yet, she frames it as a question. If I may put words in her mouth once more, it is something like this: "Is this the way that I can find peace? If so, here it is. Here are all the names and psychoses. Perhaps they can lead you to a sort of peace amid your own trauma."

And with that prologue, the album moves to a more contained and "close up" look at religion as a tool for that journey. And the findings are, naturally, both positive and negative.

"Baba"

"Baba" is the first liturgical song on the album, grouping many of its observations into "I've seen . . . " and "How long/soon/much?" This is perhaps the defining trait of the album. Most of the tracks use some form of liturgy (by which I mean repetition and form). It is appropriate that we first encounter that liturgy in the song that introduces spirituality and religion. This album is a sort of liturgy of self for Morissette, as she lays out All Parts of her identity and begins to group and contrast them.

With "Baba," Alanis introduces one of the album's major themes: spirituality. Watching her spiritual journey from *Jagged Little Pill* (1995) to *Such Pretty Forks in the Road* (2020) is fascinating. On *JLP*, she includes a song ("Forgiven") about her negative experience of growing up Catholic and her jaded rejection of religion. *SFIJ* finds the songwriter in a very different space following a trip to India. (We seem to have Marcus to thank for that . . . but we won't meet him for another ten tunes.) While she remains skeptical of religion, she devotes at least three full songs to her growing spirituality, and it colors many of the others. By *Such Pretty Forks in the Road*, she is praying on her kitchen floor to "Her," who is compared to Mary, Shakti, and Kali (who is mentioned in "Baba" with one of the album's best word tricks: "I've heard them chanting 'Kali, Kali' franti-Kali"). Clearly, by 2020, Morissette had settled into a syncretic belief system that sounds a lot like religion. Listening to "Her," in fact, I can't help feeling that Alanis understands the

"Baba"

Christian God very well—she just hasn't made the jump to identifying it as the Christ which her upbringing soured her on...but she's so close.

"Baba" has a lot in common with "Forgiven," in that it describes shallow and selfish behavior by those who claim to be religious. (On "These R the Thoughts," a track which didn't make the cut for *SFIJ*, she wonders "Why do you say you are spiritual, yet you treat people like shit? How can you say you're close to God, and yet you talk behind my back?") The vital shift between the albums is that, in *SFIJ*, Morissette seems to be looking on from the side of the authentically spiritual. And, as these quotes show, her major criterion for determining true spirituality is integrity and good works. She knows it by its fruit. How many of us devoted Christians could pass this strictly biblical test?

As with almost all of her songs, "Baba" offers a lot to Christians who have begun to lose sight of the Gospel amid church culture. There are some scriptural parallels here—the psalmist cries "How long?"; we are encouraged to "count the cost" of our faith—but Alanis presents these ideas in their twisted versions. Perhaps we could imagine the lyrics in our context thus:

> How long will this take, Jesus?
> How soon will I be holy?
> How much will this cost, pastor?
> How much longer until you completely absolve me?

There are so many great comparisons to be made here. Do we worship God at our rituals, or do we desire to be emotionally raised to false heights? While these wannabe Buddhists are condemned for leaving their families in search of nirvana, Christ warns us that we must be prepared to do the same to follow him. Many (perhaps all) of us have had to give up our addictions at Christ's altar. Many (perhaps all) of us have repeated rote Scripture with elitism. While we do not believe that God is in our own essence, we know that we are in his image and that he lives within us—but how often do we seem to overlook those facts? (D. J. Marotta gets very close to Morissette's wording when he writes, "According to the story of the Christian Bible, your neighbor is a remarkable creature. He or she is an eternal image-bearer of God that is uniquely imbued with dignity, honor, freedom, and worth. Your neighbor, in their very essence, possesses an aspect of divinity."[1]) If Alanis were watching us, what lyrics would she write? I'm afraid many would find their righteousness "mixed without loving compassion" and their hopes set on "instant salvation."

The last line of the third verse offers us a choice of interpretations. What is that mysterious smile a sign of? Is the guru laughing at the students' earnest hypocrisy? Is he enjoying his exalted status? What is the attitude of the religious figure in this song? We sense the narrator's frustration amid belief, and we are shown the supplicants' self-serving going-through-of-the-motions, but what about Baba himself? The song leaves us with his unexplained smile—a strong ending. But it is not quite the ending. The song truly ends with a reprise of the bridge: Alanis singing "Ave Maria" over and over. If you thought she was only talking about Buddhism, take care: she sees us.

---

1. Lansing and Marotta, *Our Church Speaks*, 191.

"Thank U"

THE ALBUM'S BREAKOUT SINGLE, "Thank U" picks up the baton from "Baba" by taking the liturgical structure even further as the singer turns from the hypocrisy of her fellow pilgrims in India to examine what has made her burgeoning faith a surer foundation than theirs.

The song alternates between lessons she hopes to bring home and apply to her life (the how-bouts, we might call them) and gratitude to the circumstances that allowed her to learn them (the thank-yous).

If we start by examining the thank-yous, we can compile a curious list:

- India
- terror
- disillusionment
- frailty
- consequence
- silence
- providence
- nothingness
- clarity

I Too Once Thought . . .

This grouping, suitably, covers a broad spectrum of things normally considered "good" and "bad." Once again, we see bothness. God himself (for I think we can agree that he is the one who teaches spiritual truth) uses All Parts of himself and his world to get our attention and teach us about himself. We might more easily link spiritual growth to things like silence, clarity, and providence than to traditionally negative experiences such as terror, disillusionment, and frailty. But anyone who has been through God's schooling and revelation should quickly realize the parts these things have played. Without our weakness, we have no need to fall into his strength. Without our fear, we would never choose to. And without consequence, we would never learn how.

We can also relate to the breadth of lessons God teaches, from stewardship of our body to clear-eyed reckoning with the world's tactics of distraction. Morissette tells us the necessity of both "enjoying the moment" and "bawling your eyes out." As Rainer Maria Rilke suggests in *The Book of Hours*, "Let everything happen to you: beauty and terror. Just keep going, for no feeling is final."[1]

Some may look askance at the line "how good it feels to finally forgive you," for Alanis will continue to write five more albums in which she fights to give her abuser forgiveness. But the true process of forgiveness is one of continued and intentional release of our enemies. I am thankful to Alanis for modeling this hard process in the public sphere—succeeding and failing but always pressing toward true forgiveness.

The very next line in "Thank U" sheds more light on this endeavor: "grieving it all one at a time." When we are bent under the heavy mass of another's wounding, forgiveness often feels impossible. How can we forgive a lifetime of abuse? We can't—not all at once. But one by one, God is faithful to bring up the memories of our slow destruction. Just as the offense covers many instances, we must grant many doses of forgiveness. When we commit to follow God's unveiling of our pain, he gently but insistently brings us to one wound at a time.

---

1. Rilke, *Book of Hours*, 62.

"Thank U"

As we reach the third verse (and the line "How 'bout remembering your divinity"), we must again alter the wording in our head if we are to find the lesson for our life. "How 'bout remembering God's divinity" is a good start, but we must also understand the ways in which the Spirit's presence within us unites us with Christ, allowing God to pardon us through his atonement. How 'bout remembering our worth to the true divinity? (Also, recall the D. J. Marotta quote from our discussion of "Baba.")

The verse ends with one of my favorite lyrics: "How 'bout not equating death with stopping." Think of what it means to hear a popstar so simply express that which our culture so strongly denies: death does not equal stopping—not for any of us. The world fears death above all else, but for believers, it is not something to dread. Far from the end of our life, death signals its true beginning. We so often forget that we are all immortal creatures. It is an immortal you sit next to on the bus. It is an immortal you curse from your car window. It is an immortal you face in the mirror each day. Do not equate death with stopping. How often we need that reminder!

"Are You Still Mad"

With all of this multiplicity, it can get hard to really know anyone or anything. I can vouch for this, because both Alanis and I are INFJs according to the Myers-Briggs personality test. This happens to be the rarest type, and in some ways, I am thankful that more of the world's population doesn't have to live in this world as an INFJ. Those of us given that designation take in copious amounts of data at all times, through all inputs, and we see meaning in everything. It's wonderful but exhausting!

The amount and complexity of this constant meaning-full information necessitates an ordering system. I compulsively (and joyfully) curate lists. Morissette does something similar with her lyrics. The liturgy and litany that is stamped everywhere on *Supposed Former Infatuation Junkie* is a way of making sense out of the bombardment of her experience without losing any part of it. Within the strictures of a structure, All Parts can be accounted for, and only by airing that great multiplicity can we feel at all known. (Similarly, within the framework of therapy, there is safety to let the bothness be.)

In "Are You Still Mad," Alanis's lyrics put forth a litany of problematic relationship dynamics followed by the repeated admission that these things produced a lasting and justified anger in her ex. The refrain—"Of course you are"—is not only repeated but layered. The chorus is a sort of fugue song in which the words

"Are You Still Mad"

remain the same but we hear the singer's voice inflecting them with two different melodies.

Strangely, this is where the song starts to bulge with meaning, instead of the far more verbose and varied verses. Several interpretive possibilities arise here. I have read excursuses that project a taunting and sarcastic tone to all of the lyrics. In this model, the narrator needles her ex with the question, "Are you still mad?" while rattling through all of the complaints he brought up when they were together. This is supposed to be a sort of rehearsal of the negative parts of their relationship used as torture. (In other words, he is being sent to the dungeon to learn how to make peace with his days in the dungeon.)

I don't accept this reading. Nothing in the chosen wording or the performance of the song suggests sarcasm to me. Instead, I see this more plainly as one of those *mea culpas* with which *SFIJ* is littered. It is possible that during the verses the narrator takes offense at the possibility of a lingering grudge, but by the time she reaches the chorus, she hears herself recounting her mistakes and softens into the "Of course you are."

It is also possible that the entire litany is just that: a list of things done wrong. I think of Christ's little liturgy with Peter post-resurrection. "Do you love me?" is bad enough once, but three times drives the point home while simultaneously granting penance and absolution for Peter's denials. Similarly, the dual chorus may be saying "How could you have gotten over it yet?" on one level and "You certainly have a right to be angry." on the other. (I find it revealing that the song's title does not include the expected question mark.)

It also reminds me of the moment of revelation in which the sins we have been justifying stand bare and wretched in the light. This is not only the first step of recovery—to admit that you need help—but the beginning of any surrender to God. It is the initial T in TULIP. It is the first line of the sinner's prayer. It remains the bedrock of our dependence on God throughout our lives.

And perhaps the bottom line is that all of these meanings coexist. How often do we speak words that carry multiple

I Too Once Thought . . .

connotations? Naturally, we have conflicting feelings about our relationships. We feel a bothness that we don't always recognize. You will find that voicing your confession to your brothers and sisters in the Body is a very different thing than releasing it in your prayer closet. But this communal rhythm of repentance is the very process in which the Body is healed.

Interestingly, Morissette has placed this song next to "Sympathetic Character," which further complicates the affair.

"Sympathetic Character"

"Sympathetic Character" is almost a mirror image of "Are You Still Mad." Here, in an awkward but specific rhythm that gives a feeling of stammering or rushing through a prepared speech, Alanis explains the fears that led to her relational failures from the previous song. But in this instance, there is no need to ask if she is still mad.

The words come pouring out as she explicates her behavior. The verses and chorus of "Sympathetic Character" are one of the clearest instances of the problematized identity we're discussing. In her "I was afraid of . . . " statements, Alanis is revealing a huge amount of varied information about herself and the man she is writing to. We see by her confession the vulnerable areas of her soul as well as a secondhand portrait of her ex, whom we assume merits at least some of the expressed terror. Then, in the "You were my . . . " statements, another side of both lovers is revealed: she names the multiplicity of his relation to her while revealing a lot about her own needs and expectations.

However, while the chorus lends the song its name, the idea of a sympathetic character is most clearly explored in the pre-chorus. We all want someone we can identify with, whether that be in literature (where the titular phrase originated) or life. But how can we see the similarities between these two lovers with just the verses and chorus? The man described in the former seems hardly to merit the attachments in the latter.

I Too Once Thought . . .

The pre-chorus identifies what they have in common: rage, pain, and hell. (Imagine what those wedding vows would sound like.) They may both feel these intense emotions, but they deal with them in very different ways. The man seems to radiate his anger and pain, creating a chaotic and dangerous demeanor. Alanis, characteristically, tries to contain and dampen her negative attributes. (We will see this pattern of making way for the other throughout the album and come to understand some of the origins of her choices and fears as it draws to a close.)

This song is the explosion that happens when Alanis's boiling pot reaches critical pressure. Her ordering impulse allows her to keep her fears and her romanticizations separate, with the pre-chorus between them. With the information set out in this way, it becomes unclear how the two categories can coexist. "If I were so full of fear," she might say, "how did you become my anchor, savior, and brother?"

The answer to that question has to reckon with the contradictions of the human soul. In many ways, it was because she feared this man that she held him so closely. She responded to the fear he elicited in her by turning to him for deliverance. It doesn't parse logically, but the human heart often doesn't. The album (and this book about the album) are about just that. As we continue through *Supposed Former Infatuation Junkie*, we eventually find something of a key in the final song. The lyrical parallels are also strong between that song and this. But in "Your Congratulations," the man inspiring the fear is (I believe) Alanis's father. No wonder she has grown to be drawn to similar men and to feel a strange comfort in their instability.

There is another subtle shade of meaning to the title. When we read or listen to these lyrics, which character do we sympathize with? Alanis is the true sympathetic character. Her pre-chorus statement of their similarity is more than an explanation of her affections; it is a warning to the abuser that she can fight back in kind, if need be. She has discovered sympathy for her own predicament instead of for her lover.

"Sympathetic Character"

The song ends beautifully with a realization so shocking that she must restate it. The problem in the relationship was, ultimately, not the man's reckless nature but her interpretation of that nature as worthy of adulation. Her elevation of him to savior status was the issue.

"That I Would Be Good"

"That I Would Be Good" is something of a prayer, a reminder, a defiant assertion, a hope, and a realization. This versatility comes from the words that are not there: the words that are missing from the start of each line. This simple, elegant, and profound use of syntax has once again complicated what might have been a far simpler—and far inferior—song.

The lyrics are a mantra, a liturgy, a rehearsal of what can easily be forgotten. Our culture (in 1998 or now) often sends us messages that directly contradict these assertions. (Or it is more correct to say these lyrics contradict the messages of our society?)

Some of these "if" phrases are more predictable: assurances about human worth being unchanged by appearance, weight, approval, relationship status, or worldly success. I recently went bankrupt, and I can assure you that, far from discrediting me (there's a pun there if you want it), it improved me. Other lines are more interesting, and I'd like to take a look at some.

The song starts with the line "That I would be good even if I did nothing." In the twenty-first-century West, this may be the most controversial line in the whole song. If there is one thing our culture hates, it's doing nothing. We need to be always moving up and out, finding a side hustle, seizing every single day, and being the best that we can be, darn it! Even the church struggles here, with the commandment about the Sabbath being one of the most often broken. In fact, congregations across the Western world are dying from duty, when we are called to contemplation. In recent years, the spiritual disciplines of silence and solitude have been coming to the forefront of our discussions for exactly this reason. (Again, I relate personally, since being disabled has kept me from having a job, that thing from which my identity is supposed to flow. A stranger's first question is usually "What do you do?")

The third line hits a similar vein, bringing up health. Sickness is often treated as if it were weakness or moral dissolution in our country. The same people *carpe*-ing all those *diems* live in fear of getting sick simply because of the way it forces you to do nothing. Alanis takes it a step further: what if she "stayed sick"? This phrase holds a double meaning for me. It certainly refers to illness or disability that is irreversible, fatal, or incurable. It includes every child born with a diagnosis. But it also challenges the same American will-do spirit alluded to in the first line. When someone falls sick, we may not judge them for it, but if a sick person chooses not to fight the sickness with ever-increasing futility, we likely will dust off our gavel. Is the person who is battling their disease of more worth than the one who is succumbing? Perhaps we should ask ourselves why we are so eager to stave off death. Remember, it isn't the same as stopping.

The reference to "my hair and my youth" is straight from the meteoric rise to superstardom Alanis underwent after releasing *Jagged Little Pill*. She was identified by both of these things: her long "grunge" hair and her "angry young woman" precocity. This sense of becoming yesterday's model also rings through the lines about being queen and all-knowing.

It's in the chorus, though, that the lyrics hit their hardest. Here, she sings not of circumstances (like sickness) but of behavior. She pushes the question to the brink, asking her audience if they would think less of her for unhealthy behavior. These things are often choices, and we feel very content judging people for their choices. Constantly pigeonholed by the anger present in "You Oughta Know," Alanis fought hard at this point in her career to break out of that narrow characterization. "Yes, I was angry. I still am angry, but never singularly so," she stated in an interview.[1] Here, she asks the listener if they will love her even when she's fuming. "No feeling is final,"[2] and therefore basing our opinion of someone on an emotion makes little sense.

Still, she pushes a little bit further, invoking a word often used to demonize women: clingy. What about then? Does that affect my worth or the way I should be treated? And, in one last thrust, she goes all the way. What can't our culture forgive? Insanity. We have always had a habit of putting our mentally ill where we don't have to see them. "Is that too far?" Alanis seems to ask. "If so, I have one more. I'll be just fine without *you*."

The real power of "That I Would Be Good" is not in its pressing of buttons or pushing of prejudices. It is that we get the sense that Morissette is singing these words to herself, reminding herself of both her many sides and her singular worth.

---

1. Morissette, *iTunes Originals*, track 2.
2. Rilke, *Book of Hours*, 62.

"The Couch"

WITH TRACK SEVEN, ALANIS circles back to the stream-of-consciousness she employed on "Front Row." Now, instead of sitting in the front row, she is sitting on a therapist's couch. The lyrics here do not display layering, liturgy, or litany. This time, that liturgical repetition is in the music, which repeats a melodic strain relentlessly. There is no chorus. There is, as well, an uncertain number of speakers.

This is, for the first time, true stream-of-consciousness in the tradition of Virginia Woolf. The words are again fecund and seem to overflow the form. However, the musical line acts as the ordering system when the words cannot. In what has become a trademark of Morissette's songwriting, the words do not seem to be written to the melody but forcibly inserted. Pauses take place in the middle of thoughts and even words. The emphasis and rhythm of the language is distorted.

The nature of therapy is well-represented by this odd structure. In the safe space of the therapist's couch, the thoughts and words and feelings are freed to spill out in whatever paroxysms and waterfalls they come up in. It is the space—the medium—of the couch/office/relationship that holds all of that chaos, and the therapist who sorts, orders, synthesizes, and offers it back. The medium here is the melody.

One of the common ways that Alanis approaches generative honesty is to sit at the piano, play a repeating line, and free-write vocally into a recorder. The familiarity and continuity of the cycling phrase become a comforting matrix that can free her mind to tap into on-the-spot creativity (often an outward result of behind-the-scenes introspection). In a very true way, the piano bench takes the place of the couch, allowing the flow of phrases that have not been censored and shaped by the conscious mind.

For me, "The Couch" was the moment that I fell in love with *SFIJ*. Just as the prose of Woolf absorbs me, this style of free-floating voice made sense to me. Perhaps my mind noticed an affinity of process that reminded me of my creative writing. I write in the space between waking and sleeping. It's a precarious balance, but it quiets the inner critic and brings the realm of symbol and dream closer to the surface. It also couldn't hurt that I have spent my life in therapy. As I grow older, this song only becomes more relatable, and I often sing it repeatedly while driving.

In "The Couch," we cannot identify an Alanis-narrator. Interestingly, none of the speakers in this song seems to be female, with only one verse spoken to "my sweet daughter." Elsewhere, the therapist is referred to with male pronouns, and it's hard to tell if this change to the daughter is an example of off-couch therapy, undergone by talking through issues with one's family, or some more obscure reference. Many of the personae that flow throughout this song are unclear. Sometimes, it seems that "you" is referring to the patient. But, then why does the second verse refer to the speaker(s) as "us"? Who is the "you" of the final verse?

Identity here is not only complex but truly multiple. The exits and entrances of the multiple speakers are muddled, leading to a truly problematized sense of a self. The idea that our selves are a gestalt of those we have known helps me make sense of these lyrics. My parents are part of me; my abusers are part of me. Every story we have been told is incorporated into our identity to a minuscule or monumental degree.

This clearly recalls Internal Family Systems. In that therapeutic method, a central and essential "Self" presides over a large number of "parts." While these parts are not separate personalities, they often want distinct and different things. Although Morissette had not come across IFS at the time of this album, her natural paradigms of imaging the self were not far from that framework.

Described by its pioneer, Dr. Richard Schwartz, IFS makes a distinction between parts: there are "exiles," which are parts of us that remain in moments of childhood trauma, and there are "managers" or "firefighters," which seek to meet the needs of the exiles and manage their pain and distress. The key to this theory is that the firefighters are so busy controlling the exiles' internal blazes that they are not free to perform the natural psychological functions for which they were made. Hope comes through the healing of the exiles and the liberation of the managers to return to their appointed tasks.[1]

Schwartz parallels this inner system with our outer families. The same dynamics are at play in familial relationships. Some members have bent out of their intended roles to accommodate another. Clashes of interest and a difference in profound triggers create conflict and chaos. Thus it is within us, too, says Schwartz.

This approach is similar to the work I have benefited from and helped administer as a part of the healing prayer ministry Living Waters—with one huge difference. We would also visit those moments of childhood trauma and seek to heal the wounds we find there, but whereas IFS puts the capital-S Self in the healing role, Living Waters goes straight to the source and invites the Father, Son and Holy Ghost to administer the work. In speaking about Internal Family Systems, Alanis Morissette has made the connection that the religious call the Self "God," and while this is a total misunderstanding of God, it is also about one step away from biblical Christianity. She need only discover that "Her," the Self, and God are all names for a divine person made incarnate through Jesus Christ.

While I would love to inspect every line of "The Couch," I think it is better left to the contemplation of the reader/listener. I don't want to limit the connections God might make for them personally. But I want to address the word "magistery," used in the final verse. For years, I tried to believe that Alanis was singing

---

1. Morissette, *Conversations*, 2017.

"majesty"—and most lyrics you find will transliterate it that way—but there is a clear 'r' sound in her pronunciation. Finally, I came across the word "magistery," which makes perfect sense in this context (even though it is a somewhat obsolete word). Merriam Webster's Dictionary tells me that it can mean "mastership or authority" (the Self's desire to own all its parts) or "a principle of nature having transmuting or curative powers" (the Self's ability to heal its exiles and turn its misled managers into their proper faculties).

Finally, I pass on what I have found to be true: the last two lines of this song make an excellent prayer: "You are wise. You are warm. You are courageous. You are big. And I love you more now than I ever have in my whole life."

"Can't Not"

Now that Morissette is herself firmly seated on the couch, we are privy to a sort of self-counseling session in "Can't Not." Here, she unloads all of her (surprise: conflicting) feelings about the media scrutiny of her abrupt and extensive fame after *Jagged Little Pill*. The "you" in this song refers to her interlocutors, both individually and *en masse*.

It's again important to remember the ways in which the world constructed an idea of Alanis as a person-brand. She was seen as transgressive, angry, dark, unpredictable, and completely unbothered by what anyone said to or about her. She was, as she joked in the fifth track of *Jagged Little Pill*, "Miss Thang," and she could see "Right Through You."

Of course, this third-party packaging of her persona was incredibly selective, ignoring lighthearted tracks on *JLP* like "Head Over Feet," "You Learn," and "Hand in My Pocket," which all enjoyed constant radio play. But their levity never outweighed "You Oughta Know" to balance her media image.

Supposed Former Infatuation Junkie provides even more vulnerable songs. Hearing all of the apologies and confessions on this album was actually shocking at the time. Yet this song starts with the admission, "I'd be lying if I said I was completely unscathed." (Later, she takes this revelation further in "One," which is almost entirely confession and apology.) This human Alanis was very hard for people to fit into their fixed minds: an emotionally open, raw, and vulnerable woman laying out her wrongs (and the wrongs done to her) in the constant search for order and reconciliation—with others and within her self.

The song's opening verse explores the contradiction of the title's double negative. Caught in a catch-22, the singer doesn't know if she should speak out about the media's misconceptions or try to brush them off. Either way, she realizes, the gossipmongers get more grist for the mill to grind her bones for bread. This unfathomable paradox is so ludicrous that she couldn't explain it to a child. The thought makes her think of having someone (a family, a child) completely on her side and able to see and love her in all her multiplicity. . .a safety net which she must then confess that she lacks.

And yet there's that paradox: she can't get her music around the world without the spiteful help of the press. She can't disappear from the public eye and continue her career. But, then again, she can't stand to see her words misrepresented one more time.

The effect of her delivery of "Would I be whining if I said I needed a hug?" shatters both our ideas about her character and our hearts. In verse two, she speaks to her fans, saying that fame and public adoration do not a person fill. What does it profit a woman to gain the whole world and never get a hug? But, again, she silences herself with the thought that she invited these people in, and she really does love and need them. So what if they don't really know who she is? So what if they're slowly crushing her?

During the next chorus, her patience and silence break. She can only be who she is, weaknesses and all. Is there shame in that? Why do they even care about her private life? What is the point of these questions?

The music slows down and thins out to a music-box delicacy in the bridge, when she unleashes the questions she would like to ask her interviewers. In this explosion of anger (isn't that exactly what they expected of her?), the placidity of the music is her defense against the chaos. Calm down. Breathe. She sounds so fragile during this bridge, upset at her falling into the endless cycle again.

"Can't Not"

Her playground analogy adds to this sense of an ashamed inner child.

This, according to Internal Family Systems, is exactly what she finds. Realizing and repeating that she had no agency to escape the paradox, the Self begins to heal that exile. As her confidence and compassion grow stronger, she turns out of herself and begins to see what this type of culture is doing to the world. Now she can laugh at their underestimation of her. Now she can warn us that the media is a blind guide. Now she can ask everyone to help address the problem, because it is not hers alone. And systemic change only happens when people are willing to question their own opinions.

The song ends with a sort of benign recrimination of herself for allowing the bloodhound press this power in her life. Why isn't she Miss Thang after all, safe in her impenetrable skin? And why does it have to work this way? The final answer is all but inaudible as it slips beneath the pulsing layers of music: it just can't not be this way.

"UR"

Here, in the exact center of the album, we find a song called "UR." (No, it's not about Abram being called out of Ur...but it is about the action of leaving home. Just like in "Thank U," the writer is pioneering textspeak without knowing it by replacing words with letters.)

This song marks an important moment in the album. Appropriately, it is in the middle of an album about Alanis's complex identity, because it is a song in which she tells her younger self who "you are." It is also a sonic rest, as the orchestration is light in every way. After the yearning expressed in "Thank U" and "That I Would Be Good," there is little frisson in this tune, lyrically or musically. Could it be that at her center, surrounded by all the questions and problems, Morissette is simply a hopeful child heading out into the world with a song? (Let me put it this way: when else do we hear Alanis singing "la-da-da-da-da"?)

The first verse is another of Morissette's clever *bon mots*. As I mentioned in the introduction, up to this point she has been "keeping the books" by filling in all the figures and trying to make them balance in a Self. Now, with a joyful lilt in her voice, she commands that the books be destroyed. These books/journals/songs are so full of such unfiltered revelation that they would provide the hounding media a year's worth of stories, at least.

With this freeing immolation, she turns to the past, where she is being tutored in her new record deal and cajoled into a

"UR"

performing career. In the third verse, she is traveling from her home in Ontario down to New York City to, presumably, get the ball rolling on her U.S. contract. She is nervous but insouciant, declaring her fears at customs with a joking swagger.

I trust that I needn't say much about the choruses in this song, given the theme of this book. Here, in the center of it all, she spells it out clearly. It's as if, having healed some childhood trauma at the end of "Can't Not," she is pausing to bask in the good of her growing up years. This is the eye of her identity storm, and it is almost cloyingly sunny...until verse four.

The mood is still light, but here she is acknowledging the difficult and damaged parts of her childhood and celebrating those that have been healed and made her stronger. Unlike the rest of the song, which is sung to young Alanis by older Alanis, this verse introduces new voices.

A straightforward reading would assume that these are supportive friends whom she has kept at arm's length. ("Reeling in and then spitting out" is a theme in all of Alanis's music and seems to typify her approach to friendship.) But, just for fun, let's look at this verse through the lens of IFS. In that light, these voices might represent the many parts of Alanis that have been trying to put out the fire only to be beaten back by the wounded child exile.

Straightforward and humorous, "UR" is a wonderful intermission in *SFIJ*. It is also a harbinger of lighter things to come. The second half of the album contains heavy songs, like the first half, but they are joined with a larger number of joyful and lighthearted songs.

"I Was Hoping"

AFTER THE CENTERPIECE OF "UR," Side B opens with "I Was Hoping," one of the most compelling songs both musically and lyrically. This is one of those songs which is structured by a musical motif, like "The Couch," but here we also see a short chorus that uses the familiar technique of lyrical liturgy.

The song features both models because it is narrated, in a sense, by two Alanises—one who recounts the memories of her interaction with the subject and one who comments (almost as an intrusive voice) on the lost hopes she held for the relationship. It is probably safe to assume that her connection with the "you" of this song—or potential connection—was romantic (despite the subject's mention of a wife), but the chorus's lyrics could be interpreted as part of a desired platonic intimacy. The final line, then ("I was hoping we could be creamy together."), is either the one obscene reference on the album or a metaphor for a smooth and harmonious friendship.

Just as demonstrated on "The Couch," the lyrics of "I Was Hoping" are delivered quickly and in an unusual rhythm, aping the uncomfortable reengagement with a lost partner. (Some of this is represented for us in the irregular enjambment of the verses.) This technique also gives the song energy and a magnetic quality, causing us to lean in to catch what she is saying.

The verses are beautifully invoked vignettes that trace the (likely short) arc of a relationship that doesn't take flight. The first

"I Was Hoping"

verse recalls a private conversation (or perhaps a few) by highlighting the sticking points where the narrator felt friction in the growing bond. Verse two looks like a self-contained episode, but it is split at the end, with a chorus interrupting what is really a grouping of three lines: "I too once thought I was owed something. I too thought that when proved wrong, I lost somehow. And I too once thought life was cruel."

Clearly, those three lines mean a lot to me (check the title page of this book), and I think they act as the core of the song. The first statement describes the verse which it concludes. The second describes the discussion from the first verse. The third opens the final verse as a thesis statement.

Before I give free reign to my love of these lines, let's look at them in relation to the rest of the song. This track reveals Morissette's less praiseworthy sides. Throughout, she is peevish and annoyed and judging her partner from a self-satisfied place—what we would today call "virtue signaling." And then, in the final line before the last chorus, she makes the confession that she intentionally modulated her tone to cover up this (supposed) judgment.

While I do not know what order Alanis wrote these songs in with her songwriting partner Glen Ballard, this seems like it might be an early composition. The language gives the impression that Morissette is unaware of her poor treatment of the subject. (The very next song will act as an apology.) The singer's newfound spirituality seems immature here and mostly based in proscribed behavior and clichés that have not been thought through. But we have never accepted these things as counterfeit faith ourselves, right? We never put ourselves under the law in enthusiastic legalism or clung to slogans that could never hold a fraction of what Christians truly believe. Never. Moving on.

The inherent contradictions involved in a multiplicity of identity are in the open here. "I don't believe in. . .right or wrong, good or bad," but (the subtext says) you're clearly both wrong and bad. In fact, in the core triumvirate of "I once thought" statements, we see the unironic acknowledgment of being "proved wrong," something she supposedly doesn't believe in. For someone who doesn't equate death with stopping, her advice to this man seems oddly confident that he's "not going to die anytime soon." And, in the delicious second verse, the singer pats herself on the back for not saying what's on her mind, but she doesn't seem to be concerned that it still comes to the forefront of her thoughts.

Is there any wonder that the next song starts by saying, "I am the biggest hypocrite"?

But, let me turn again to my cherished triumvirate of lyrics. The reason my book title came from these statements is the way that each clause acknowledges multiple selves. "I too once thought" assumes a current "I" who has learned better and a past one who "once thought" differently. It is also an I-statement that supposes a "you" with the word "too." It is simultaneously apologetic, gently chastising, and teaching. It gives credence to the abandoned idea (what was once thought) by sympathetically admitting one's own former belief in the same. And yet it celebrates growth within oneself while encouraging it within the other. It is a retraction—something often embarrassing but essential.

I run these three lines through my head often. They have proven excellent reminders for me. Am I owed something? Anything? I can rely on God's promises, but even they might not become evident during my time on Earth. Does God really owe me anything? Happiness? Security? Freedom from pain? Family? Health? A "good" life? I once thought so. (The surest of Christ's promises? "In this world you will have trouble.")

I also once believed that a conversation was a contest, that it was shameful to change my opinion, and that "losing" was a purely negative thing. Too many people in our world hide these untruths in their hearts. We are a culture that refuses to apologize, be swayed by the arguments of others, or cede alpha dog status. We must never admit defeat. But when we are in the wrong, we must learn to welcome what we call defeat, and we must strip that concept of its stigma. Because if we don't, we will only feed this world of people who talk constantly and never really listen. It is a joyful thing to discover the truth! We must not let our competitive society keep us from embracing it when it comes along.

"I Was Hoping"

Lastly, I still often think life is cruel. Who could begin to prove that it isn't? Ask me most days, and I will tell you that the world is cruel, people are cruel, nature is cruel, and life itself is cruel. But perhaps I need to be proven wrong. Perhaps I need to finish the promise of Jesus I quoted before.

"I have told you these things, so that in me you may have peace. In this world you will have trouble. But take heart! I have overcome the world."[1]

---

1. John 16:33

"One"

As I said, this next song acts as an apology for the hypocrisy in the previous one. Here, Alanis takes a look at Miss Thang and realizes that she's not the greatest person. (Need I point out the maturity evident in these lyrics that any number of today's celebrities could stand to take to heart?)

This song is open and vulnerable, not ashamed to apologize for shameful behavior. And it covers a lot of ground succinctly. She has been jealous, pretentious, separatist, hypocritical, and even (disgusted at the idea of being) average. Many celebrities seem fond of rolling out the "not a role model" sign. But, as Billie Eilish (a clear successor to Morissette's queendom) reminds us, even though you didn't ask for this power, you have it now, so don't abuse it. A more helpful and honest sign would be one that reads "still human." And, to flip around an old saying, what is more human than erring?

"One" contains some brilliant lyrics, from "surely we both can't be amazing" to "I've gotten candy for my self-interest." The best lines, though, are the couplet that ends the first verse: "Heaven forbid I be criticized. Heaven forbid I be ignored." Sadly, in Alanis's world it must often seem like one or the other. As long as she speaks up, releases music, lends her voice to charities, and so on, she is sure to be criticized by some segment of the world population. These lines might act as another great mantra to remind ourselves that neither criticism nor disregard are forms of "losing"—just like

"One"

being proved wrong. They tell us more about the other person than they do about ourselves.

But we must, of course, contend with the chorus of "One" if we are to say anything meaningful about the song. I think we can safely link "we actually are one" with "overlooking God in their own essence" and other similar phrases to infer that Alanis is working with a largely Buddhist spirituality at this point. However—as I hope I've demonstrated already—we need not swallow Buddhism to learn from these lyrics.

Firstly, I think it is in keeping with the theme of this book to think about how the idea of all things being one presupposes a vast complexity within that one. Scale back the assertion, and we can see how a person is also a collection of countless diverse parts. Yet the important thing to notice is that, even amidst all those selves, the person is still a unified singular being. The admission of a multiplicity of identity does not change the fact that each of us is in some state of harmony and uniqueness. Somehow, all those parts synthesize to make a distinct person.

On a more spiritual note, we should all feel the sting of conviction when we hear these words. We don't believe that all things are literally one, but we very much do preach that the church, at least, is one Body. (And in that sense, all of God's human children are united in the *Imago Dei* and our stewardship of humanity and the Earth.)

I think that we too often content ourselves with a vague assent to the idea of the Body of Christ. It looks good on paper, at any rate. But I have found the true acceptance of our unity and the type of life that takes seriously the idea of one hurt Christian harming the entire Body to be sadly rare. I become aware of this whenever I do witness the Body living or moving in unity, because I experience a little shock of recognition. If the church were moving beyond theory in this area, it would be the times of disunity that would stand out. Unfortunately, that disunity is the norm.

I am not only speaking of schisms and interdenominational disagreements here. The brokenness of the Body is all too evident at that scale, but it is no less present in your local congregation.

I Too Once Thought . . .

The Body of Christ is more than a pretty metaphor; it is a powerful spiritual reality. And that reality is a mess in our gatherings. The enemy you are called to love needn't be a godless world leader. They are probably sitting two pews behind you. They are probably sitting in your very heart.

We can learn from Internal Family Systems here, even if its practitioners have taken it too far. Do we not harbor traitors within? Do we not recognize our own voice in those surprisingly hateful thoughts that seem to come out of nowhere? Do we honestly even pretend that we don't see all the Do Not Disturb signs in our spirit? God is a gentleman: he will not knock down those doors except in extreme need. It is not some godlike Self that we need to invite into our places of hurt and hatred. It is the God already waiting at the doors.

"Would Not Come"

MADE UP OF SELF-TOLD lies in the verses and vain pursuits in the chorus, "Would Not Come" never specifies the unspoken "it" of the title. This type of omission is a running theme on the album. We do not know, for example, what clause precedes the title phrase in "That I Would Be Good." We can't properly assign the pronouns in "The Couch." As we'll see, the next song uses aliases to obscure the identities of its subjects. Throughout the Alanis Morissette oeuvre, we find examples of withheld information, the most talked about being the identity of the man who shows up continually as her abusive ex-lover.

In the lyrics of this song, she daydreams about being "aloof" and "elusive." And yet, what marks Morissette's work more than anything else is the sheer amount of information she does divulge. She may refuse to scratch the public's prurient itch, but I know no other songwriter who brings us so closely into her head with devastating honesty. Her lyrics are extensions of her ever-growing collection of diaries and journals. These are the books she wants to burn in "UR" for the "incriminating evidence" of their "names and neuroses," but while she doesn't divulge names (and thereby infringe on the privacy of others), she is shockingly open about the neuroses.

It is this obsessive confessional honesty that makes her lyrics so universally powerful. A timeworn adage holds that the more specific your writing is, the more universal its impact will be. Or,

I Too Once Thought . . .

as Alanis herself says in an interview, "The personal is the political. The personal is the global."[1]

And in "Would Not Come," Alanis gets personal. The Teacher of Ecclesiastes keeps things almost vague in comparison, but they cover the same ground. The Teacher first turns to wisdom, knowledge, madness, and folly. Alanis tells herself that she must accumulate knowledge. Neither seeker finds satisfaction. They next looked to pleasure and wealth. The Teacher builds and buys and drinks. Alanis chooses vodka, seduction, orgasms, shopping, eating, and travel. Toil is meaningless to the Teacher, and Morissette responds with her money ("tinsel") and fame, her productivity and heroism. Even the poor and the spiritual find their plans thwarted. Alanis renunciates, starves herself, stays silent. There is no reward.

(Yet, notice the many scattered desires and beliefs and lies and fears that make up this one, complex Alanis.)

Of course, "Would Not Come" *does* not come to a conclusion. The song ends with the singer still in pursuit of "it." The most that can be said is that she has perhaps learned that the lies she has been telling herself are indeed lies. After all, she chooses to go with vulnerability despite her fears, as evidenced by her overflowing self-revelation on this—and every—album.

And this highlights the thing standing in her way. Ecclesiastes ends by telling us to fear God and follow his commands, as is our duty. One can sense Alanis groping after a law to follow and a god to serve, but I doubt that she would think to fear that god or follow his/her commands out of sheer duty. Our society is not prone to walk toward duty or cherish fear.

We do these things because we have encountered a person instead of a mere god. God's outpouring of honesty is even more verbose than Alanis's—it fills sixty-six books, none of which can be burned. Left with an emptiness and a sense that there is something she has been chasing, Alanis moves on to the next song (which could be seen as a record of this same search in her relationships).

Perhaps the key thing here is that whatever "it" is, it will never come. But we have encountered the "he" that did, quite literally,

---

1. Morissette, *iTunes Originals*, track 20.

"Would Not Come"

come. By the end of the album (as we will see), she will have stumbled upon the fact that what she needs is a father. I continue to pray that Alanis may recognize him, too.

"Unsent"

AT THIS POINT IN an album that has been so focused on self, Alanis turns outward once again (where she started with "Front Row"). Her quest for self-definition hasn't let up, though. Having exhausted all of her experiences and introspection, she now looks to others in an attempt to understand not only who she is but who she would like to be.

The first of these other-focused songs is "Unsent," which (based on the title) may be seen as an aborted first try to figure herself out through her relationships. This song stands out from most of the album due to its simple instrumentation and relatively light tone. It is another of those songs that relies on musical repetition to create order through liturgy. (For some reason, these are the songs that grab me most.) While there is little repetition in the lyrics, they do follow a form: letters to old boyfriends.

Thanks to the demo recording of this song, we know the identities (or sometimes just names) of the men in question: musicians Dave Matthews (rechristened Matthew), The Foo Fighters's Taylor Hawkins (whose verse was cut), and Christian Lane from the band Loud Lucy (renamed Lou), as well as first-name-only entries Eric (the song's Jonathan), Terry (Terrence), and Marc (Marcus).

By going over her history with each ex, Alanis begins to take inventory of what each man gave to her. This realization that the people in her life have shaped who she is sets in motion the final phase of the album. We can now add these deposits from others

"Unsent"

to the expanding list of parts swirling around within our titular supposed former infatuation junkie.

This tour through the boyfriends of times past also forms a sort of roadmap of Alanis's development over the years. The Jonathan verse chronicles her bad-boy phase, during which she sought out damaged and dangerous men. (Might this be the timeframe of her infamous older abuser?) Terrence acts as a direct counterbalance to this chaos, providing her with support and care that allowed her to heal from her past relationship and move forward in her life. (She also drops a mention of another couch here, in the verse which details her most therapeutic relationship: "I remember how beautiful it was to fall asleep on your couch and cry in front of you for the first time." This is, suitably, also the hardest lyric on the album to sing due to its rapidity and cramped insertion into the rhythm. After all, for Alanis, this vulnerability must be the hardest thing to admit.) Marcus is credited with her growing interest in the spiritual, and Lou represents her first adult romance, which teaches through pain and regret. (Once again, though, we see seemingly contradictory impulses coexisting, as she also expresses mature care and respect for Lou.)

The main takeaway of "Unsent" is the way in which other people can become parts of our own identity out of care, injury, or education. This theme continues through the end of the album.

"So Pure"

AND NOW, A DANCE break. This may be the song that comes closest to not belonging on the album, but it was a clear commercial hit that they knew would do well in clubs. So here it is. It's a simple song, musically and lyrically, but that is the point. It is called "So Pure," after all.

After thirteen songs (more than most other albums) about the untraceable complexity of identity, cascading with endless lyrics and employing a host of unconventional sounds in the orchestration, we get a song of pure joy and bouncing beats. A dance song about dancing. (Why are there so many of those? And rock songs about rock music?)

In our narrative of the search for identity, "So Pure" follows the decision in the previous track to seek answers by looking to others. One can imagine our hypothetical Alanis contemplatively strumming "Unsent" before deciding to finally take that break she's been agonizing over and go dancing. There, she meets the "you" of "So Pure." This doesn't sound like a prelude to romance (although it could be), and the prominence of trance music leads me to suspect (with a reliance on stereotype that goes against the entire mission of the album) that this is a gay man with whom she strikes up a casual affinity. (But, then again, there is that "knot in my stomach and lump in my throat.")

Suddenly, faced with someone who is uninhibited and jocund—who can live in laughter without lists—in an environment

"So Pure"

that does not lend itself to immediate deep conversation (her default get-to-know-you), Alanis sees what she longs to be: purely and simply herself in the present moment. INFJ that she is, such a goal is not in line with her personality. In a sense, nothing can be "pure" (undiluted and simple) in her world. Everything has meaning, remember. She can't even get through this fun little song without starting to unpack the possible meanings in this dynamic. She can't simply be in jealous awe of this person. She immediately is rhapsodizing about "cosmic tears." Clearly, she thinks, "you" is "relevant" (Will she herself prove to still be relevant when this second U.S. album comes out?) and "luminous" (Could she ever shine so brightly?).

There isn't a lot more to say about this song. In it, we find the album title, appropriately positioned after a song about all her previous infatuations and in the middle of what may be a new one. But she is not in full introspective mode. Something in "you" brings out her energetic, fun side. She jokes that they could solve the world's problems over tea.

And then, to continue our little scenario, she comes home to find those problems assailing her in the form of a panicked phone message, driving the album toward its conclusion.

"Joining You"

THE CULMINATION OF ALL the album's thoughts on identity, "Joining You" acts as the climax of *Supposed Former Infatuation Junkie*. It is a dramatic, urgent composition set with truly profound lyrics. "Joining You" may be my favorite song—period—because Alanis is speaking directly to me with words that I often need to hear.

The song is a monologue, with narrative verses and a chorus that melds layering, liturgy, and litany to make a strong thesis statement about the problem of ever knowing who we are. The closest Morissette can get to describing what we are is to list things that we are not—or not merely. A full human is too complex to identify and transcends any descriptors we may apply. And that, the song says, may be the only hope we have in this world.

The song's story involves the singer getting a panicked message from a friend whose daughter has started talking about suicide. (The young person is never given any gendered descriptors. I'm just extrapolating from the opening greeting of "darlin'.") While I believe that this young woman is real, she can also stand in for a younger—or simply less composed—Alanis. She also reminds us of IFS's wounded parts: the exiles. And, certainly, she allows the singer to speak to the audience in a direct address.

This young woman is very like the Alanis we have gotten to know over the course of this album. She is "intense" and "uncomfortable," searching for meaning in everything around her and hoping to "find God" in the process. This is a woman who is asking

"Joining You"

the same questions about identity that have filled each song we've looked at.

When forced to give an answer to someone in the same position as herself, Morissette is pushed to find the kernel of her thoughts and put it into words. Without this outward, other-focused need, she would likely have stayed in her own musings longer than necessary. Crisis galvanizes revelation.

And what is that revelation? What is the lesson the songwriter finds that she has learned over the course of this collection? She starts by acknowledging the reasons why suicide seems so attractive. As someone who has lived through periods of desperately wanting to die, I am disarmed and warmed by this openness.

Discussion of suicide carries a huge stigma in our culture, as well as reactionary laws about mandatory reporting. I understand the need for these laws, but at my lowest, they feel like a trap. Every person in a mentoring role is bound by these rules. And that almost feels like a weaponization of my safe relationships. The very people with whom I felt like I could discuss my distress seem to me—even as an adult—to be forced into the role of informer. And since mental illness scares most people, I am often silent for fear of being locked away.

But Alanis has centered her entire response around the assertion not only that she understands but that she feels the same overwhelming hopelessness when she looks at any one part of herself or the world. Over and over, she replies that she would join this woman in her choice of death if things were truly as hopeless as that. That is a powerful stance, even from a disembodied voice on my stereo.

But what hope does Alanis cite as worth living for? She doesn't. She instead implies that any simplistic reading of things is dreadful but not complete. We are not merely our "bodies" and "rejections" and "afflictions." They are part of us. We are not defined by "our leaders," "our obsessions," or "our emotions." All of these things are only parts, just as Internal Family Systems speaks about identity as a collection of parts.

I Too Once Thought . . .

There is something beyond and behind all of that—something much more complex. Alanis is not able (yet) to explain what this intricacy is. Perhaps it is IFS's Self. Perhaps it is the image of God coursing through our molecules. Perhaps it is just a recognition that any thinking about ourselves is reductionist.

I learned this lesson while walking at dusk on a hill near my rural home. As I walked, I was praying about the messages culture was sending me about who I was—especially as a man. I felt flattened and pigeonholed even by people who loved me, and I worried that the majority may be right when they set restrictive gender roles. And then a remarkable thing happened.

I felt God nudging me to stop, and I did. He asked me to look up, and I did. I saw a hill rising above me, covered in trees, rank on rank until they reached the blue-black-grey sky, a jumble of colors impossible to describe. Each tree spread out countless branches that split into endless twigs. As I looked at the tree above me against that night sky, I heard God whisper to me, "You are that complex. Don't try to define yourself so easily." Then, I looked at the entire hill rising above me, full of uncountable limbs and trunks and branches. And God said, "I am infinitely more complex than that. Trust me. There is room for you. Don't let the world steal your complexity. Bring the entire offering."

"Heart of the House"

SUPPOSED FORMER INFATUATION JUNKIE is a story, and most stories don't end at the point of climax. (True stories don't end at all.) But, having brought the album to its apex with "Joining You," Alanis adds a denouement in the form of a couplet of songs about her parents.

Having settled—for a time—the question of her identity, Morissette finds it apt to wrap up with a look at the two people who contributed to that identity more than any other. "Heart of the House" is a kind of lullaby for her mother. And, as we have come to expect, it starts by getting straight to the heart of the matter: "You are the original template. You are the original exemplary."

Looking back on her loving but under-appreciated mother, Alanis begins to ask questions about that woman's identity. She has been so driven to define her own self that she has not considered her mother as a complex woman like her. These questions and memories come in a scattershot way that is not quite stream-of-consciousness. It is as if, thinking on it for the first time, Alanis finds thoughts tripping over one another. In every other way, though, this song is interestingly free of the Three Ls. Except for the unorthodox melody and the bunching of thoughts, this is a surprisingly conventional song.

Inevitably, these thoughts boil down to the contemplation of what parts of herself she inherited from her mother. It is a sweet

I Too Once Thought . . .

way to end the album—but it is not the album's ending. This song has its opposite number, about how her relationship with her father shaped her identity, and it is the downbeat close of *SFIJ*.

"Your Congratulations"

"Your Congratulations" also uses a lullaby-like melody and simple orchestration. It is in every way the companion to "Heart of the House." And yet, the cores of the two songs could not be more different. Here, perhaps, we see part of why Morissette seems to have never given her mother's autonomy much thought. Her mother was eclipsed by a domineering stage father whose criticism crowded any other thoughts out of young Alanis's head.

The lyrical structure of this final song returns to what I have been calling liturgy: the repetition of parallel statements. These are variations on "I wouldn't have" statements. While "Heart of the House" has a sense of "I would have" in terms of appreciating her mother during her youth, the feelings surrounding her father are all negative.

Sadly, while I did not have a similar relationship with my father, I grew up having learned the same lessons. Avoid the exuberant and attention-stealing. Keep your needs and wants to yourself so as not to bother the adults. Reject those things that give you comfort; you neither need nor deserve it. Never take credit for something you've done well. Have a down-playing deflection ready for any compliment. Be a good child, because the adults don't have energy to deal with your so-called needs.

These are, as the song astutely diagnoses, the lessons of invisibility. Anything that brought attention—success, failure, noise, emotion—had to be killed at the root. Because all attention felt like negative attention. When faced with unpredictable, angry adults, the safest choice was to disappear.

For me, that meant intentionally sealing off my emotional and intellectual self and "sending it away" in times of chaos so it could not be hurt. (Is it any wonder Alanis and I need to impose order on life?) I became so adept at this that, by my middle teens, I was watching myself from a spot above and behind my body. The valuable parts of myself had taken up permanent residence in the Away.

And, just like that, my identity began to fracture. I began to discuss different parts of me by name. In IFS jargon, my managers and firefighters had taken over daily functions because my exiles were in true exile.

I say all of this to explain my identification with Alanis Morissette and especially the issues she raises on this album. I say it to show one way that identity problematizes itself. I do not mean to suggest that pain or abuse are the only ways people end up with a complex multiplicity within themselves. I suspect that it made me more aware of that complexity, but I believe that everyone experiences bothness and the intricacies of identity. We all have a lot to learn about ourselves, whether we have thought to plumb those depths or not.

But why end this beautiful album on such a downer? Couldn't "Heart of the House" and "Your Congratulations" have swapped places, giving us a more upbeat ending?

No. While both songs explore the effect of the Morissettes on their daughter, it is clear that it was Alanis's father who had the largest and most foundational impact. *Supposed Former Infatuation Junkie* is an album about the problems and multiplicity of identity, and "Your Congratulations" bears out that theme all too well.

I wonder, as well, why we feel the need to cling to happy endings. It is like those who avoid the Old Testament because it "isn't very comforting." If you're reading your Bible solely for comfort, you're missing the real seed of Christianity: acknowledgement of our fallen nature and inability to help ourselves.

"Your Congratulations"

In other words, our experience of the world has not shown happy endings to be the norm. Is it virtuous to present a softer vision of the very world we renounce at baptism? The films of Charlie Chaplin understood that a realistic ending—one of loneliness, poverty, and the need to keep traveling the road ahead of you—is not necessarily a negative ending. Just as Alanis admits her sympathy with the suicidal youngster of "Joining You," a bittersweet or unresolved ending can comfort us precisely because we are assailed with happily-ever-afters but fail to see them regularly in our own lives.

And, after everything, Alanis ends her Song of Herselves with a central truth that she has learned along the way—and learned to face squarely: all she ever wanted was her father to show his pride and love. When we come to the end of ourselves, where else do we go but to our father's house, even if it is to live as his servant?

May we all find him running to meet us.

Conclusion

WHEN I WRITE REVIEWS (which I do about three times a week), I try to craft the review to match the product. When talking about *Supposed Former Infatuation Junkie*, that means a baring of my soul and a taste of what my complex identity is made of. I owe it to Alanis to meet her on equal footing, standing on the ground she laid out. And so this has been a book with plenty of "I"s in it. But I have to admit that I am already spread throughout this album.

My therapist often (and I mean often) listens to me sum up my thoughts or feelings through Alanis Morissette lyrics, and he has long suggested that she is probably the person I feel most in synch with. Perhaps it's true. She has consistently put precise and beautiful words to my unordered emotions. Now I return the favor, in a way.

I have several hopes as I wrap up this volume. I hope that your opinions and conceptions of Alanis have altered over the course of this book. I hope that you are already queueing up *Supposed Former Infatuation Junkie* on your music device of choice. And I hope that when you listen this time that you will see the many ways that this album has been thoughtfully constructed and focused. In the language of a word processor, I hope that I have "shown invisibles."

I spent a long time choosing this book's subtitle. (The title has been filed away for years.) I didn't know what word to use to express the way this album discusses identity. It cracks it open and catalogues the strata. It starts a word web that collides with the

Conclusion

edge of the paper. More than anything, it fights against the current trend which would have us each define ourselves in the most specific words possible, squeezing into the smallest box we can and announcing our intersectional uniqueness. I finally decided on "problematizing," because all of that is indeed a problem in today's culture.

That culture loves to label things "problematic." The thing that may be most problematic to this system, though, is a warts-and-all conflicting portrait of the multitudes within an individual. In 2025, we have all been turned into managers and firefighters. We must manage our image with razors-edge clarity and put out any fires arising from the parts of us (or our past actions) that are deemed unacceptable. This leaves each of us with a hidden colony of exiles stuck in their pain. It forces us to send them further into exile for fear the cardinal sin *du jour* be discovered, cowering within us.

But in *SFIJ*, Alanis Morissette has given us a brave example of displaying All Parts (except those that would incriminate another) without the culturally required shame. Even when she has important lessons she wishes to teach, she couches them in the language of offering: how about this? When she wants to decry and deny, she gently intones, "I too once thought that." And when faced with the chaotic in herself or others, she begins with empathy, proceeds to sympathy, and leads with commonality. All the while, she models productive and honest strategies for overlaying that chaos with order, that we may take inventory and begin to heal.

What a surprising gift this work of art is! It will forever help shape and recenter my thoughts. And, darn it, Johnny, I believe you can dance to it, too!

I have singled out several passages from this album's lyrics as "mantras" which I find helpful. Don't let the Buddhist origins of that word frighten you. Throughout this reading of *SFIJ*, I have repeatedly affirmed that we can learn from alien worldviews without adopting the entirety of their precepts. I simply mean that there are pieces of text (they come from every corner of life) which prove beneficial as personal reminders of learned lessons the world

I Too Once Thought . . .

wants to beat out of us. I pray that you've found your own, and I close with the ones that serve me the best.

"How 'bout not equating death with stopping?"

"That I would be loved even when I numb myself.
That I would be good even when I am overwhelmed."

"Do you go to the dungeon
To find out how to make peace
With your days in the dungeon?"

"Sometimes it feels like highway robbery,
But sometimes it's peanuts;
I wish it could last a couple more hours."

"Heaven forbid I be criticized.
Heaven forbid I be ignored."

"If we were our indignities,
If we were our successes,
If we were our emotions, I'd be joining you."

"I too once thought I was owed something.
. . .
I too thought that when proved wrong, I lost somehow.
And I too once thought life was cruel."

"You are wise. You are warm. You are courageous. You are big.
And I love you more now than I ever have in my whole life"

Bibliography

Lansing, Ben, and D. J. Marotta. *Our Church Speaks: An Illustrated Devotional of Saints from Every Era and Place.* Downers Grove: InterVarsity, 2024.
Morissette, Alanis. "Conversation with Alanis Morissette & Richard Schwartz." *Conversations with Alanis Morissette.* October 2017, podcast.
———. *iTunes Originals—Alanis Morissette.* Recorded June 2004. Maverick, mp3.
———. *Supposed Former Infatuation Junkie.* 1998. Maverick, compact disc.
Rilke, Ranier Maria. *The Book of Hours.* Translated by Brett Alan Dewing. Independently published, 2024.

www.ingramcontent.com/pod-product-compliance
Lightning Source LLC
Chambersburg PA
CBHW071753040426
42446CB00012B/2537